DUETS FOR YOUNG VOICES

Edited, Arranged, and Composed by
Dave and Jean Perry

SHAWNEE PRESS
Vocal Library

Shawnee Press

EXCLUSIVELY DISTRIBUTED BY

HAL•LEONARD®
CORPORATION
7777 W. BLUEMOUND RD. P.O. BOX 13819 MILWAUKEE, WI 53213

Visit Shawnee Press Online at
www.shawneepress.com

Visit Hal Leonard Online at
www.halleonard.com

CONTENTS

2 BOYS OR 2 GIRLS

MAY DAY CAROL

English Spring Carol
Arranged by
DAVE *and* JEAN PERRY (ASCAP)

Anonymous

I've been a-wan-d'rin' all this night and the best part of the day, But when I come back home a-gain, I will

IB0001

A branch of _ May I

bring you here, and at your door I stand. It's just a _ sprout that's

well bud-ded out by the work of _ God's own hand. I'll _

long - er can I stay; God bless you __ all, both

long - er can I stay; God bless you all, __ both

great and __ small, And __ send you a joy - ful __ May. I'll

great and small, And __ send you a joy - ful May.

bring you a branch of May to share. I'll bring you a branch of

Bring a branch of May to share. Bring a branch of

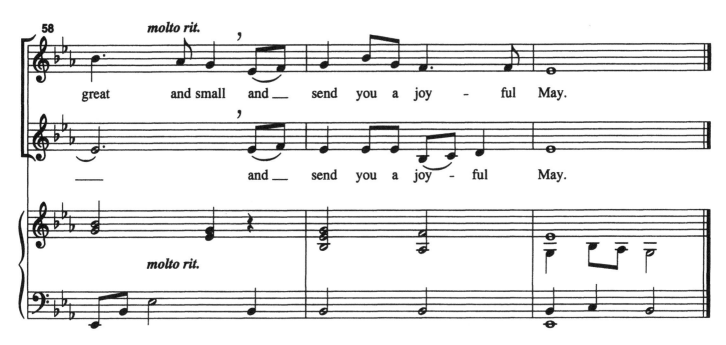

HIGH AND LOW VOICES

WILD MOUNTAIN THYME

North Ireland Folk Song
Arranged by
DAVE *and* JEAN PERRY (ASCAP)

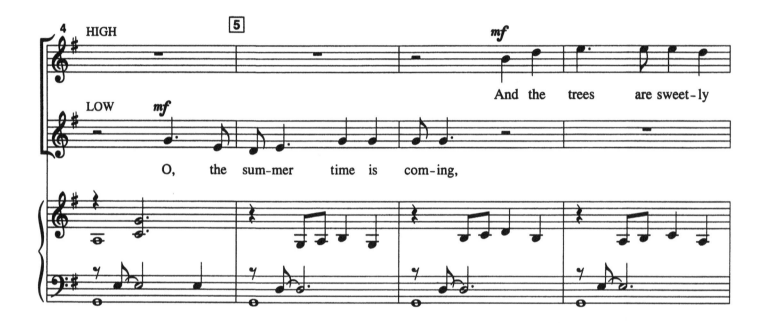

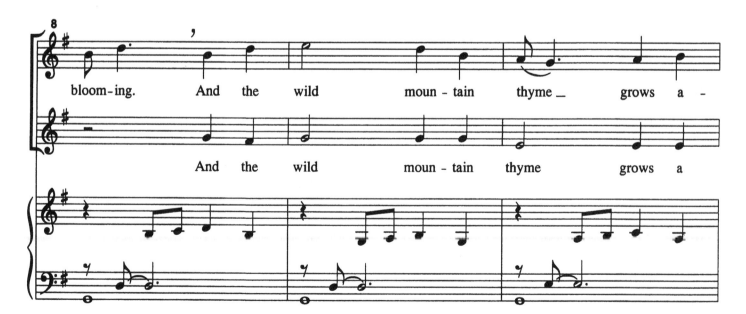

IB0001

round the pur-ple heath-er. Will you go? Will you go?

round the pur-ple heath-er. Will you go? Will you go?

And we'll all go to-geth-er, to pull wild moun-tain

And we'll all go to-geth-er, to pull wild moun-tain

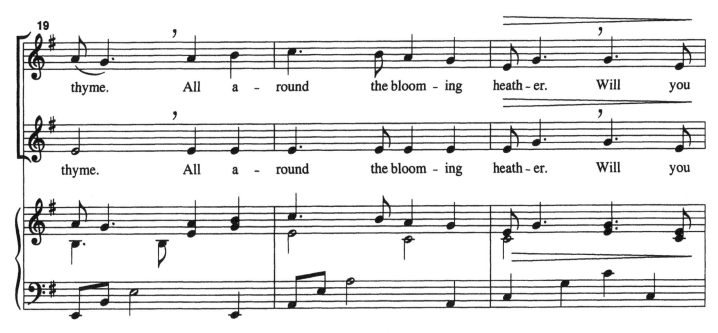

thyme. All a-round the bloom-ing heath-er. Will you

thyme. All a-round the bloom-ing heath-er. Will you

*No breath

go? Will you go? And we'll all go to-geth-er to pull

go? Will you go? And we'll all go to-geth-er to pull

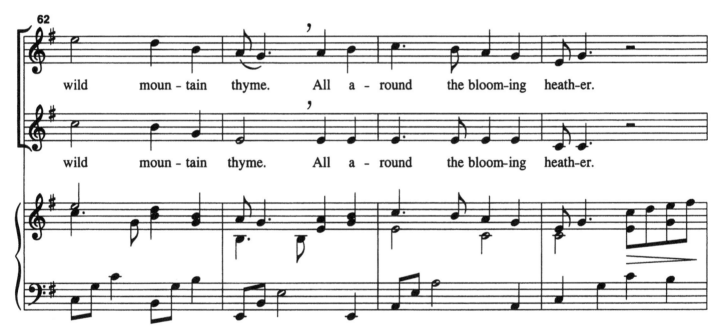

wild moun-tain thyme. All a-round the bloom-ing heath-er.

wild moun-tain thyme. All a-round the bloom-ing heath-er.

will you go, will you go?

will you go, will you go?

2 GIRLS

THE CUCKOO

Words and Music by
DAVE *and* **JEAN PERRY** (ASCAP)

IB0001

morn - ing fade in mid-day sun, And si - lence de - scends on the

warm af - ter - noon; I pause by the stream to rest __ in the

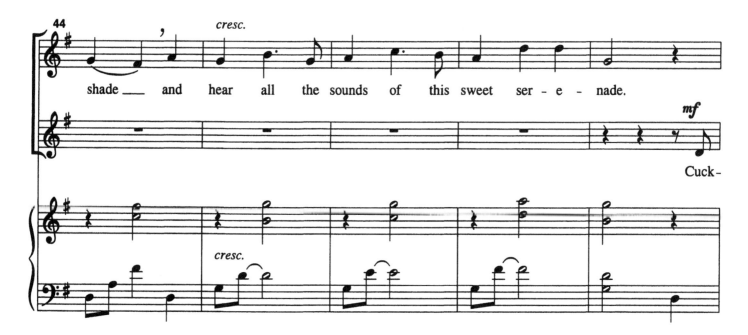

shade __ and hear all the sounds of this sweet ser - e - nade.

Cuck-

Cuck-oo, cuck-oo, cuck-oo, ____ cuck-oo. Cuck-oo,

-oo, cuck - oo, cuck - oo, ____ cuck - oo. Cuck - oo, cuck -

cuck-oo, cuck-oo, cuck - oo.

oo, cuck - oo, ____ cuck - oo.

And when day is end - ing and I can - not

And when the day draws to an end, I can no long - er

IB0001

stay; The cuck-oo sings fare-well as I'm on my way. Through

stay; The cuck-oo sings a fi-nal song to bid me on my way. Through-

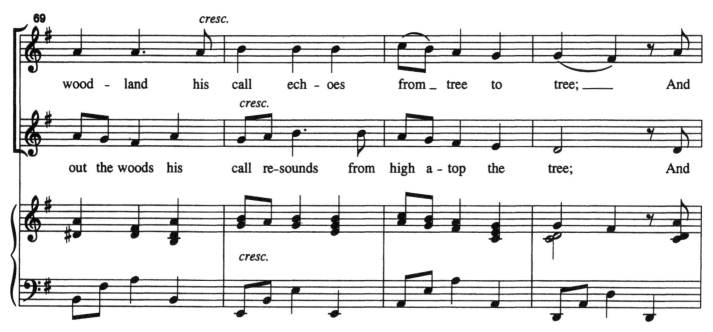

wood - land his call ech - oes from tree to tree; ____ And

out the woods his call re-sounds from high a-top the tree; And

I'll keep his song safe in my mem - o - ry.

I shall keep his song a-live with-in my mem-o - ry. Cuck-

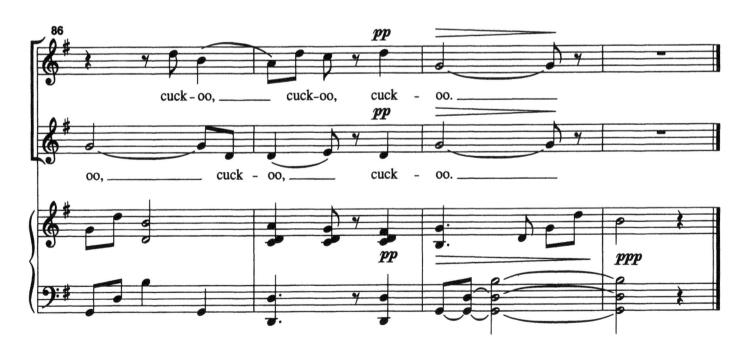

2 GIRLS

LASCIA CH'IO PIANGA

Edited and Arranged by
DAVE *and* **JEAN PERRY** (ASCAP)

Words and Music by
GEORGE FREDERICK HANDEL

24

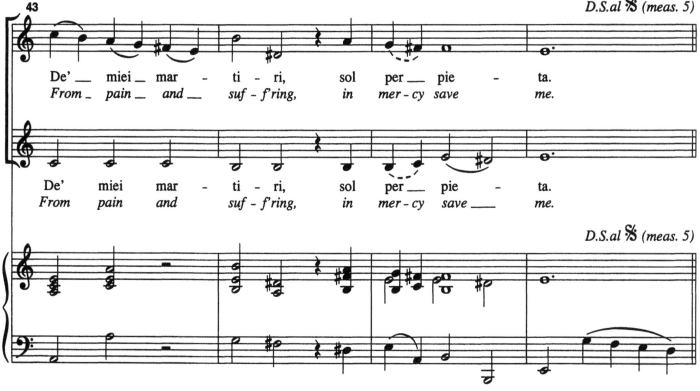

PRONUNCIATION GUIDE

Lascia ch'io pianga mia cruda sorte
Lah-sheeah keeoh peeahn-gah mee-ah kroo-dah sohr-teh
Let me weep my cruel destiny,

E che sospiri la liberta!
Eh keh soh-spee-ree lah lee-behr-tah!
And only breathe liberty!

Il duolo infranga queste ritorte
Eel doo-oh-loh een-frahn-gah kwes-teh ree-tohr-teh
The sorrow shatters the chains

De' miei martiri, sol per pieta.
Deh mee-eh-ee mahr-tee-ree, sohl pehr pee-eh-tah.
Of my sufferings out of mercy.

HIGH AND LOW VOICES

DO YOU LOVE ME?

Anonymous

Music by
DAVE *and* JEAN PERRY (ASCAP)

IB0001

Or do you not?   Do you? ___

Do you love me?   Do you? _____

Do you love me?   Do you love me?

Or do you not?

Do you love me?

Or do you not?   Or do you not?

Do you?___ You told me once.

Do you?___ Once you told me.

You told me once.

Once you told me. Once you told me.

You told me once. Do you love me?

HIGH AND LOW VOICES

YOU CAN DIG MY GRAVE

Traditional Spiritual
Arranged by
DAVE *and* JEAN PERRY (ASCAP)

sil - ver spade 'cause I ain't gon - na stay here an - y long - er. ___

sil - ver spade 'cause I ain't gon - na stay here an - y long - er. ___

There's a long, white robe in the Heav'n for me,

There's a

long, white robe in the Heav'n for me. There's a long, white robe in the

There's a long, white robe in the

Heav'n for me, and I ain't gon - na stay here an - y long - er. __

There's a star - ry crown.

In the

There's a star - ry crown.

There's a

Heav-en for me. __ In the Heav-en for me. __

star - ry crown in the Heav-en for me ___ and I ain't gon - na stay here an - y

star - ry crown Heav-en for me ___ and I ain't gon - na stay here an - y

long - er. ___

long - er. ___

There's a gold-en harp,

In the Heav-en for me. ___

O, there's a

2 BOYS OR 2 GIRLS

LOCH LOMOND

Scottish Folk Song
Arranged by
DAVE *and* JEAN PERRY (ASCAP)

IB0001

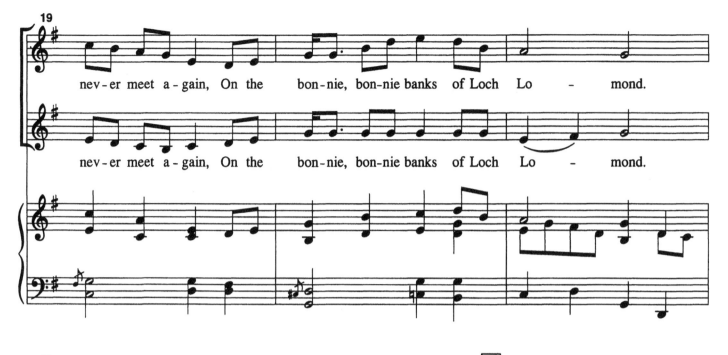

never meet a-gain, On the bon-nie, bon-nie banks of Loch Lo - mond.

never meet a-gain, On the bon-nie, bon-nie banks of Loch Lo - mond.

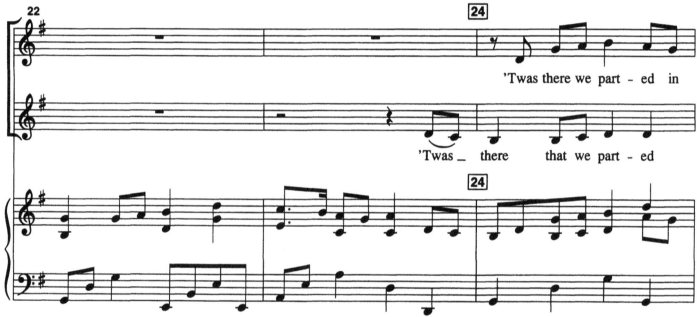

'Twas there we part - ed in

'Twas _ there that we part - ed

yon shad-y glen, the steep side of Ben Lo - mond; Where

in shad-y glen, On the steep, steep _ side of Ben Lo - mond;

MIXED DUET

PAPER OF PINS

Irish Folk Song
Arranged by
DAVE *and* JEAN PERRY (ASCAP)

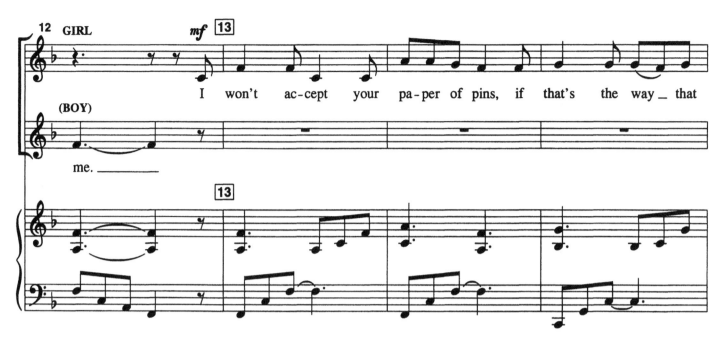

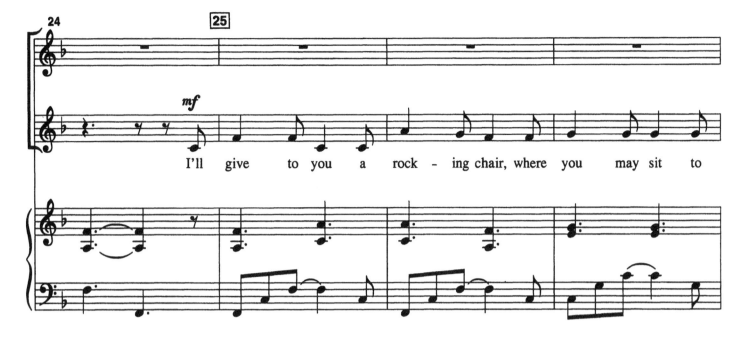

I'll give to you a rock - ing chair, where you may sit to

comb your hair, if you will mar - ry me, me, me; if you will mar - ry

I won't ac - cept your rock - ing chair, where I may sit and

me. _____

comb my hair, No, I won't mar - ry you, you, you; no, I won't mar - ry

you. _____ I'll not mar - ry.

I'll not mar - ry. I'll not mar - ry. I'll not mar - ry. I'll not mar - ry.

I'll give to you the key to my heart, that you and I may

48

I'll not mar - ry. No. No. I'll not mar - ry

nev-er de-part if you will mar-ry me, me, me; if you will mar-ry

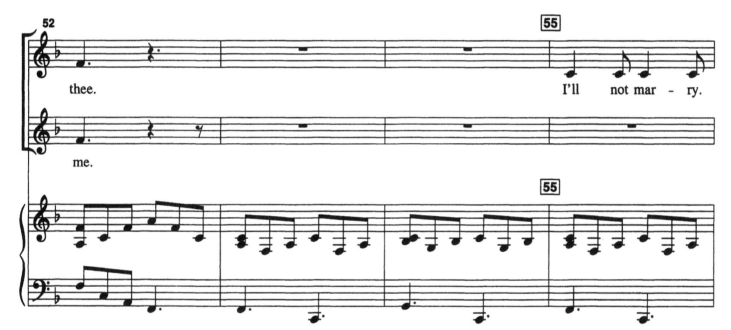

52 **55**

thee. I'll not mar - ry.

me.

55

56

I'll not mar - ry. I'll not mar - ry.

mf

I'll give to you the key to my chest, that you can have mon-ey at

May-be I'll mar - ry. Yes, _____ may-be I'll mar - ry

your re-quest, if you will mar - ry me, _____ if you will mar - ry

thee. I will ac-cept the key to your chest, that I may have mon-ey at

me.

molto rit. *slowly, with a greedy flair*

molto rit. *colla voce*

my re-quest. Yes, I will mar - ry you. ____ Yes, I will mar - ry

2 BOYS OR 2 GIRLS

PANIS ANGELICUS

English text by
DAVE *and* **JEAN PERRY**

by César Franck
Edited and arranged by
DAVE *and* **JEAN PERRY (ASCAP)**

IB0001

ge - li-cus,
prayer to Thee.

Pa - nis an - ge - li-cus,
Guide us Thy will to see.

Dat pa - nis coe - li-cus fi - gu - ris ter - mi -
Fa - ther of all, to Thee we bring our song of

Dat pa - nis coe - li-cus fi - gu - ris ter - mi -
Fa - ther of all, to Thee we bring our song of

ra - bi - lis man - du - cat Do - mi - num,
love ful-fill, *that* *we* *may* *do* *Thy will.*

O res mi - ra - bi - lis man - du - cat
Through *us* *Thy* *love ful-fill,* *that* *we* *may*

Pau - per, — pau - per, ser - vus et hu - mi - lis,
Fa *ther,— Fa* *ther, grant___ us Thy peace,* *we* *pray.*

Do - mi - num, pau - per, — ser - vus,
do Thy will. *Fa* *ther,_ grant* *us* *peace.*

PRONUNCIATION GUIDE

Panis angelicus fit panis hominum
Pah-nees ahn-jeh-lee-koos feet pah-nees hoh-mee-noom

Dat panis coelicus figuris terminum.
Daht pah-nees chay-lee-koos fee-goo-rees tehr-mee-noom.

O res mirabilis manducat Dominum,
Oh rehs mee-rah-bee-lees mahn-doo-kaht Doh-mee-noom,

Pauper, pauper, servus et humilis.
Pah-oo-pehr, pah-oo-pehr, sehr-voos eht hoo-mee-lees.